Angles Are Easy as Pie

You meet up with angles when you cut yourself a piece of pie, when you look for a good place to hide, and when you are hiking up a mountain—to mention just a few examples. ANGLES ARE EASY AS PIE offers the opportunity to learn quite a lot more about angles: how to tell the difference between big ones and small ones, how airplane pilots use them, and how they figure in such shapes as tri*angles* and rect*angles.*

Robert Froman, the author of several other popular Young Math books, has written a lucid text that will interest young readers and clarify for them a subject they must already have come across—after all, we have all wanted an even bigger piece of pie at one time or another!

Byron Barton's delightful alligator clearly understands a lot about angles, and capers through these pages carefully illustrating just what they are all about.

Angles Are Easy as Pie

by Robert Froman

illustrated by Byron Barton

THOMAS Y. CROWELL COMPANY • NEW YORK

YOUNG MATH BOOKS

Edited by Dr. Max Beberman, Director of the Committee on School Mathematics Projects, University of Illinois

BIGGER AND SMALLER

CIRCLES

COMPUTERS

THE ELLIPSE

ESTIMATION

FRACTIONS ARE PARTS OF THINGS

GRAPH GAMES

LINES, SEGMENTS, POLYGONS

LONG, SHORT, HIGH, LOW, THIN, WIDE

MATHEMATICAL GAMES FOR ONE OR TWO

ODDS AND EVENS

PROBABILITY

RIGHT ANGLES: PAPER-FOLDING GEOMETRY

RUBBER BANDS, BASEBALLS AND DOUGHNUTS:
A Book about Topology

STRAIGHT LINES, PARALLEL LINES,
PERPENDICULAR LINES

WEIGHING & BALANCING

WHAT IS SYMMETRY?

Edited by Dorothy Bloomfield, Mathematics Specialist, Bank Street College of Education

ANGLES ARE EASY AS PIE

AREA

AVERAGES

BASE FIVE

BUILDING TABLES ON TABLES:
A Book About Multiplication

EXPLORING TRIANGLES:
Paper-Folding Geometry

A GAME OF FUNCTIONS

LESS THAN NOTHING IS REALLY SOMETHING

MAPS, TRACKS, AND THE BRIDGES OF KÖNIGSBERG:
A Book About Networks

MEASURE WITH METRIC

NUMBER IDEAS THROUGH PICTURES

SHADOW GEOMETRY

SPIRALS

STATISTICS

3D, 2D, 1D

VENN DIAGRAMS

Library of Congress Cataloging in Publication Data. Froman, Robert. Angles are easy as pie. SUMMARY: Discusses facts about angles and their relationship to triangles, quadrangles, polygons, and circles. 1. Angle—Juv. lit. [1. Angle. 2. Geometry] I. Barton, Byron. II. Title. QA482.F76 516'.15 75-6608 ISBN 0-690-00916-X.

1 2 3 4 5 6 7 8 9 10

Angles Are Easy as Pie

YOUNG MATH BOOKS

Which kind of pie do you like best?
Apple?
Cherry?
Huckleberry?
Banana cream?
If you like any kind of pie, you like angles. When you cut a piece of pie, you cut an angle.

One way to describe an angle is to say that it is the opening between two lines that meet each other. When the lines meet at the center of your favorite kind of pie, the angle is delicious.

You can make angles with sticks, too.
When you put the sticks together like this,
they make a small angle.

When you put them together like this, they make a big angle.

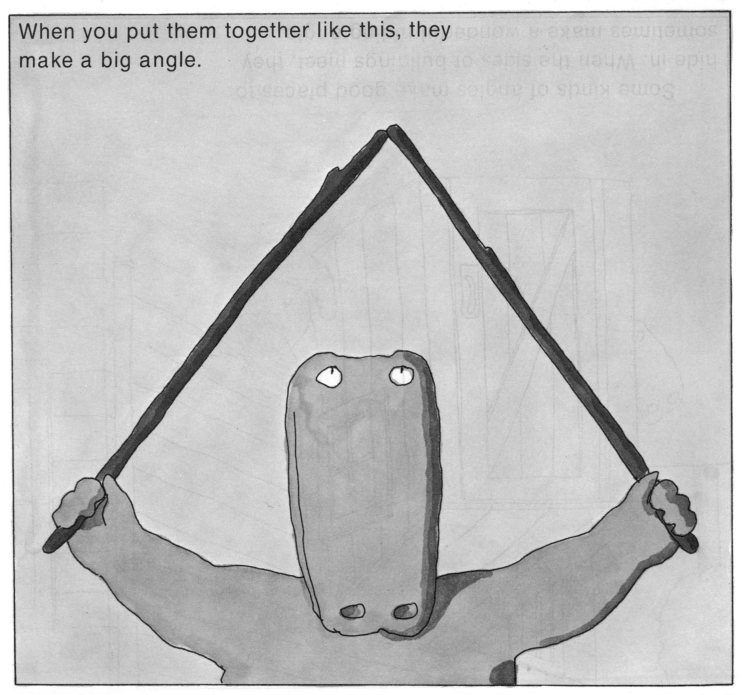

Some kinds of angles make good places to hide in. When the sides of buildings meet, they sometimes make a wonderful hiding angle.

In some attics the roof and the floor make a great hiding angle.

The size of an angle is very important when the angle is formed by the sides of your piece of pie. If it is a very small angle, the piece of pie is very small, too.

If there are four people to share a pie, each can have an angle this size.

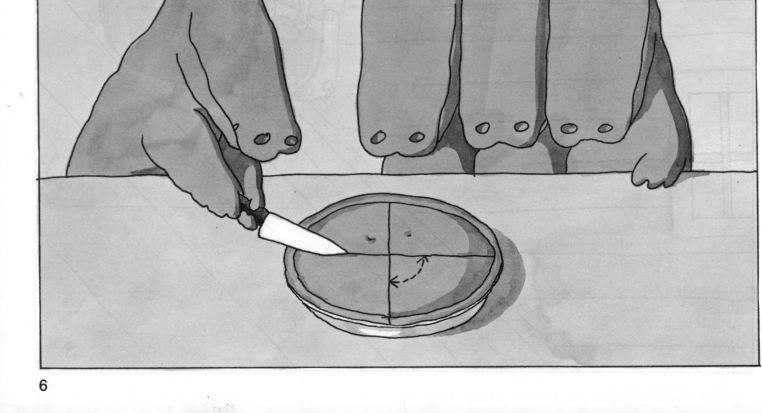

If there are six people to share it, each can have an angle this size.

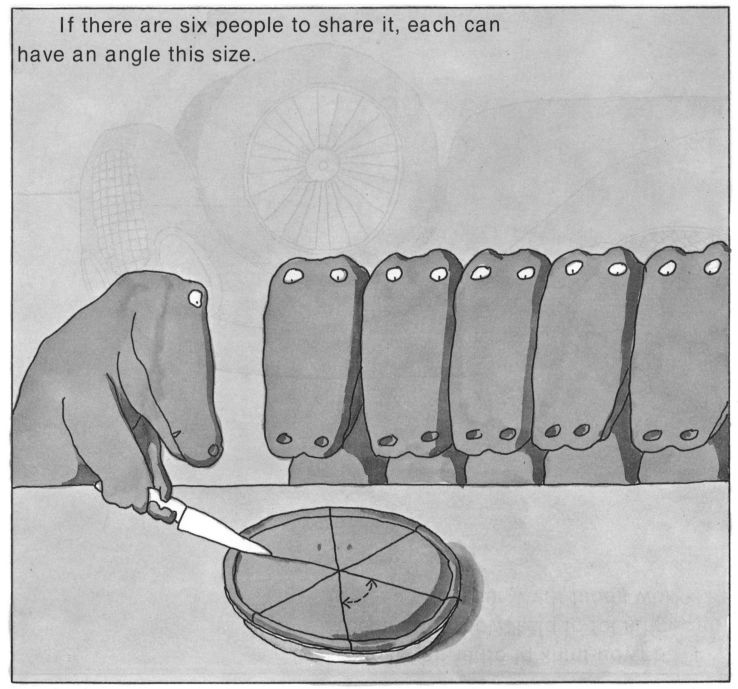

Sometimes the size of an angle tells you something you want to know.

On a sign it can tell you how steep a mountain trail is.

An angle like this means that the trail is easy to climb.

An angle like this means that it is pretty steep.

An angle like this means that it is very steep.

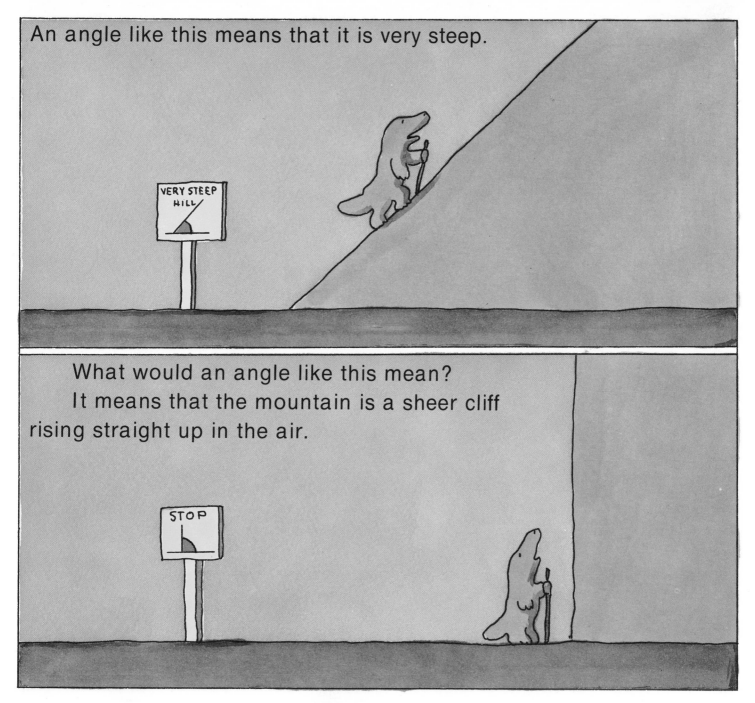

What would an angle like this mean?
It means that the mountain is a sheer cliff rising straight up in the air.

The size of an angle can tell you something about time, too.

At noon the hands of a clock are together like this.

Five minutes later the hands make an angle like this.

Ten minutes after that they make an angle like this.

The angle keeps growing until the minute hand is pointing in exactly the opposite direction from the hour hand, a little after twelve-thirty.

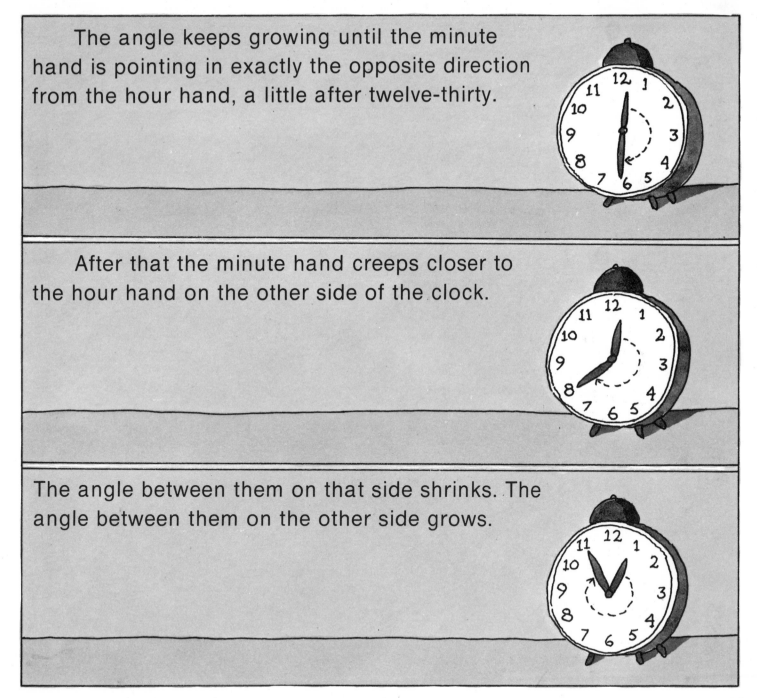

After that the minute hand creeps closer to the hour hand on the other side of the clock.

The angle between them on that side shrinks. The angle between them on the other side grows.

Clock angles can tell you something about directions in space, too.

Suppose you are in a small plane. The pilot wants you to see something.

"There's a mountain peak at twelve o'clock," he says.

Do you know where he wants you to look? Can you guess?

He wants you to look straight ahead.

Straight ahead is called "twelve o'clock," as if it is where the hour hand points at that time.

Then, suddenly, the pilot speaks again.

"Airliner," he says. "Four o'clock."

Can you guess what angle he wants you to swing your eyes through?

He wants you to swing from looking straight ahead to looking where the hour hand points at four o'clock.

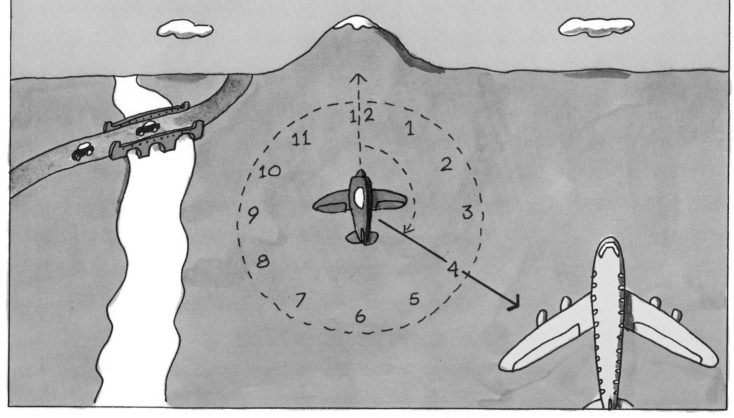

"Bridge at ten o'clock," says the pilot.
What do you do now?

You can swing all the way back past straight-ahead, or twelve o'clock, and on around to where the hour hand points at ten o'clock.

(Or you can swing around the other way past six o'clock and on up to ten o'clock.)

Can you see how big a piece of pie you would cut if its sides met in an angle like the one between four o'clock and ten o'clock?

If you cut such a piece of pie for yourself, you would be very greedy. It would be half a pie.

This half-a-pie angle is a very special angle.

For one thing, the two lines that meet to make it form one straight line.

For another thing, the half-a-pie angle is important for triangles.

"Tri-" means "three." A triangle is a figure with three angles. It also has three sides.

Here are some triangles:

Find a piece of fairly stiff paper or some thin cardboard and a pair of scissors. Cut out a triangle and number the three angles 1, 2, and 3 —like this:

Now, cut off each of these angles, like this:

And put the angles together, like this. How big a piece of pie do they add up to?

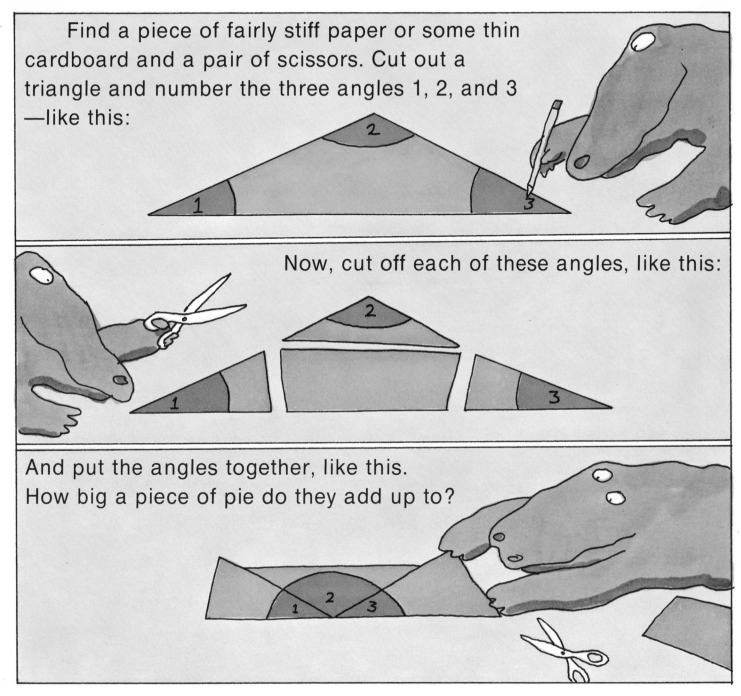

Cut out another triangle of a quite different shape. Number the angles,

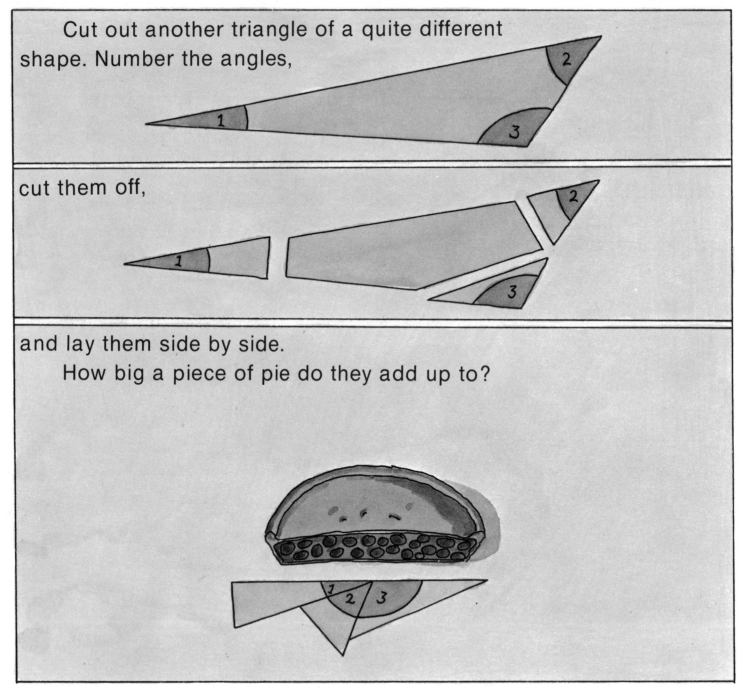

cut them off,

and lay them side by side.

How big a piece of pie do they add up to?

Try several more triangles of still different shapes.

The result always is the same. The three angles of a triangle always add up to the angle of half a pie—in other words, a straight line.

All three angles may be about the same size.

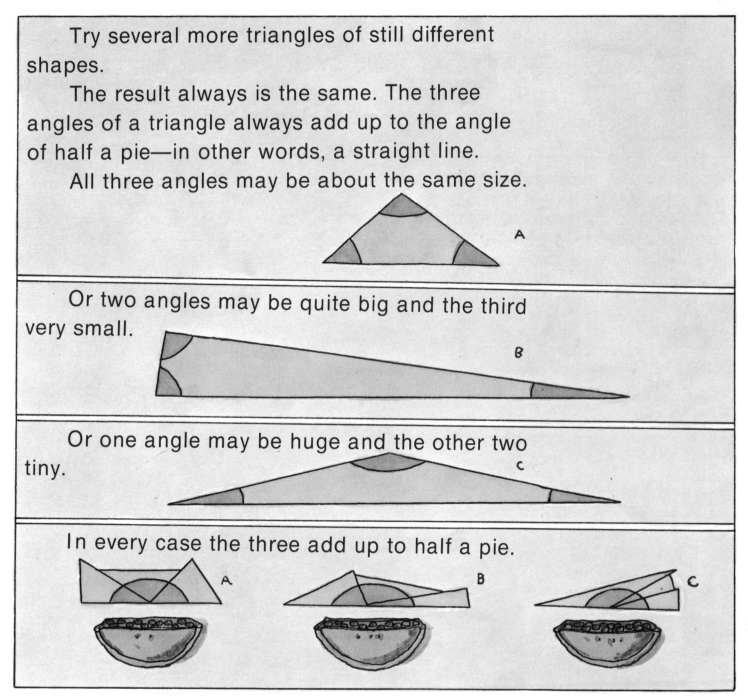

Or two angles may be quite big and the third very small.

Or one angle may be huge and the other two tiny.

In every case the three add up to half a pie.

How big an angle do you think the four angles of a four-angled figure would add up to?

If you like surprises, try the same thing you did with triangles.

Sometimes four-angled figures are called quadrangles. "Quadr-" means "four." They also have four sides, so sometimes they are called quadrilaterals. "Laterals" are "sides."

Cut out a quadrangle of any shape you like. Number the four angles like this:

Now cut them off and put them side by side, the way you did the three angles of a triangle. Are you surprised?

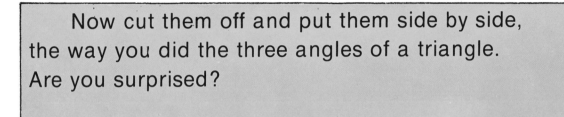

Try a few more quadrangles of different shapes, like these:

Do their angles always add up to the same size?

Yes. The four angles of a quadrangle always add up to a whole pie.

This means that these four angles add up to an angle <u>twice</u> as big as the three angles of a triangle. Those three angles add up to only half a pie.

Can you find a reason why you might expect the angles of a quadrangle to add up to an angle twice as big as the angles of a triangle?

Hint: Try dividing each of your quadrangles into two triangles.

You can always divide a quadrangle into two triangles. Just draw a line or make a scissors cut from any of the four angles to the opposite angle. Try this with several quadrangles of different shapes and sizes.

If you try a quadrangle like this, you will get another surprise.

Three of the angles in this quadrangle are very small. They do not add up to as much as half a pie. But the angle with the number 4 is very large. It is much bigger than half a pie.

Yet if you make a cut from angle 4 to angle 2, you divide this quadrangle into two triangles.

Can you think of any kinds of figures with angles besides triangles and quadrangles?

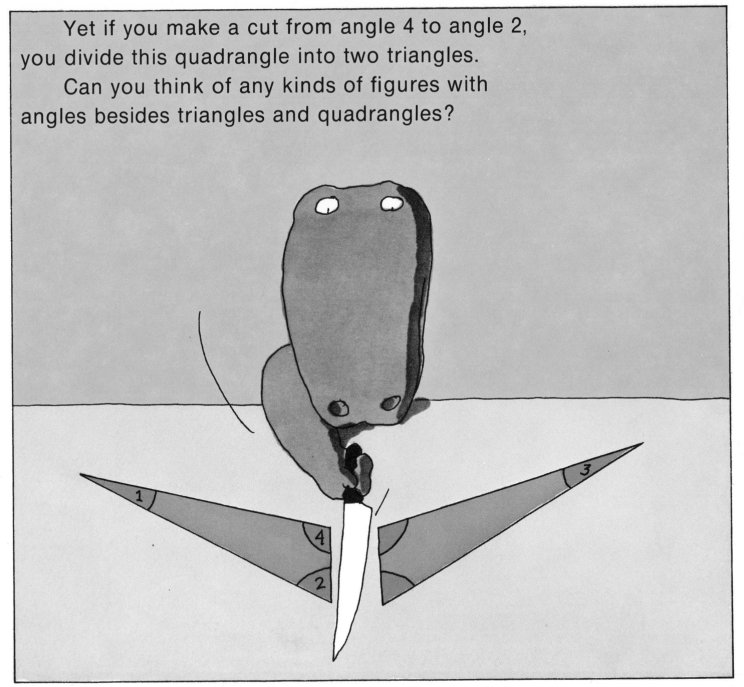

What about figures with five angles and five sides?

These figures are called pentagons. "Penta-" is from a Greek word that means "five," and "-gon" is from a Greek word that means "angle."

Cut out a big pentagon and number the angles. Then cut off the five angles and put them together. Surprised?

The five angles of a pentagon add up to a pie-and-a-half. Try a few other pentagons of different sizes and shapes, and see if the angles always add up to a pie-and-a-half.

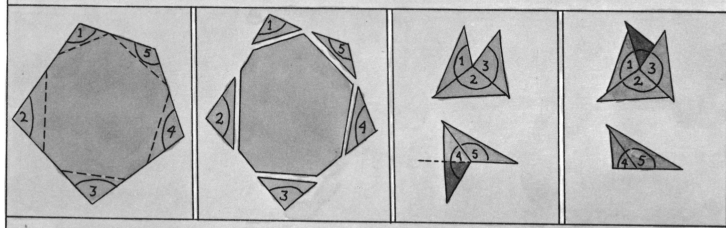

Sometimes you'll have to cut one of the five angles to see the pie-and-a-half angle clearly.

A pie-and-a-half is three times as big as the half-a-pie angle of a triangle. Can you find a reason why the angles of a pentagon add up to an angle three times as big as the angles of a triangle do?

Hint: Try dividing each of your pentagons into one triangle and one quadrangle. Then you can easily divide the quadrangle into two triangles, as you did before.

You can have fun cutting out figures with still more angles and sides, and finding out how many pies' worth of angles there is in each of them.

The six-angled figure is called a hexagon:

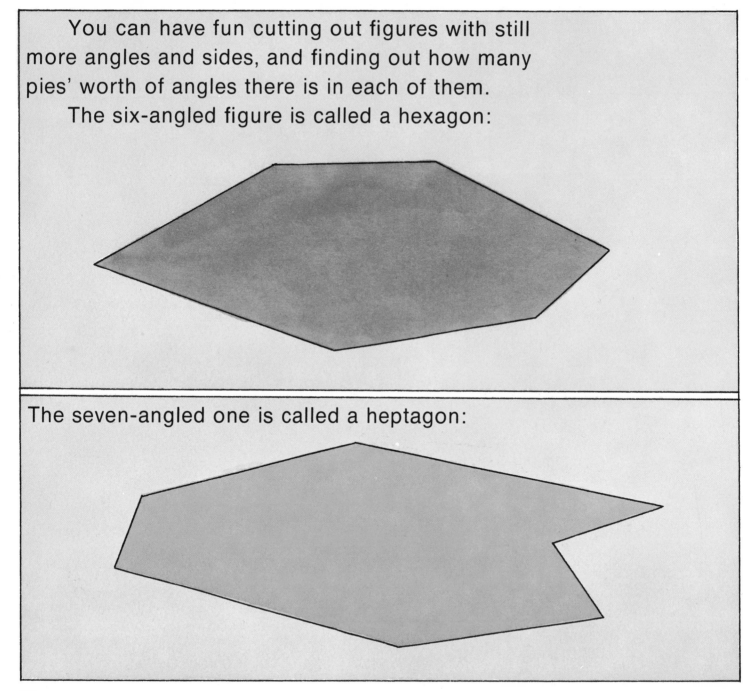

The seven-angled one is called a heptagon:

The eight-angled one is called an octagon:

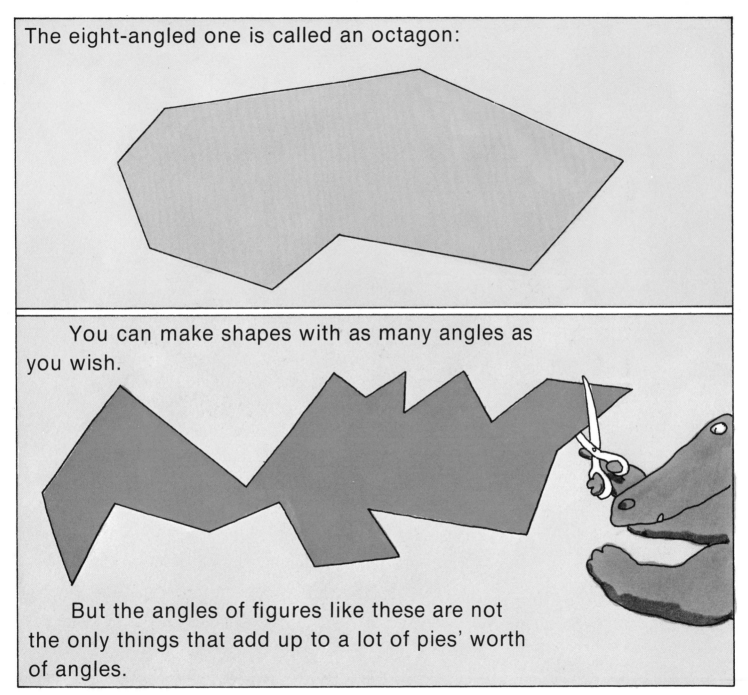

You can make shapes with as many angles as you wish.

But the angles of figures like these are not the only things that add up to a lot of pies' worth of angles.

29

The hour hand of a clock turns through two pies' worth of angles every day.

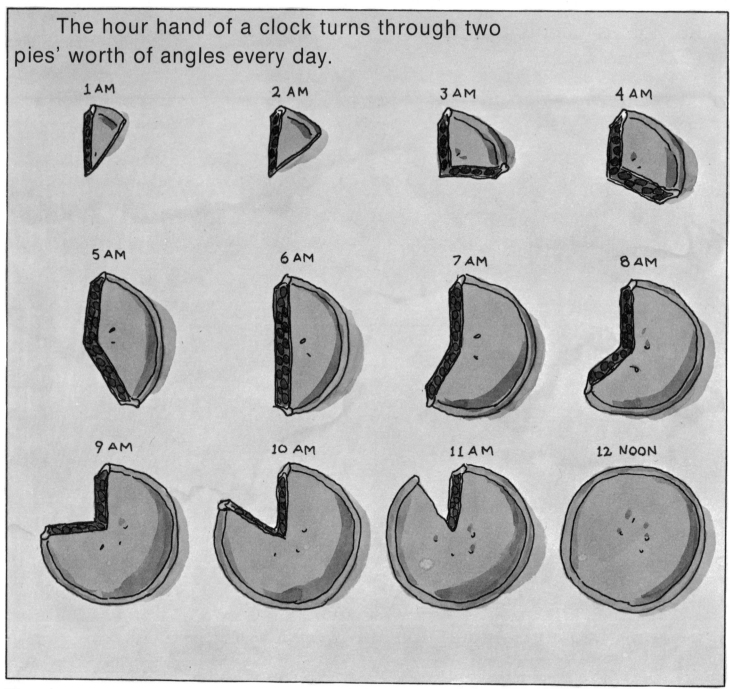

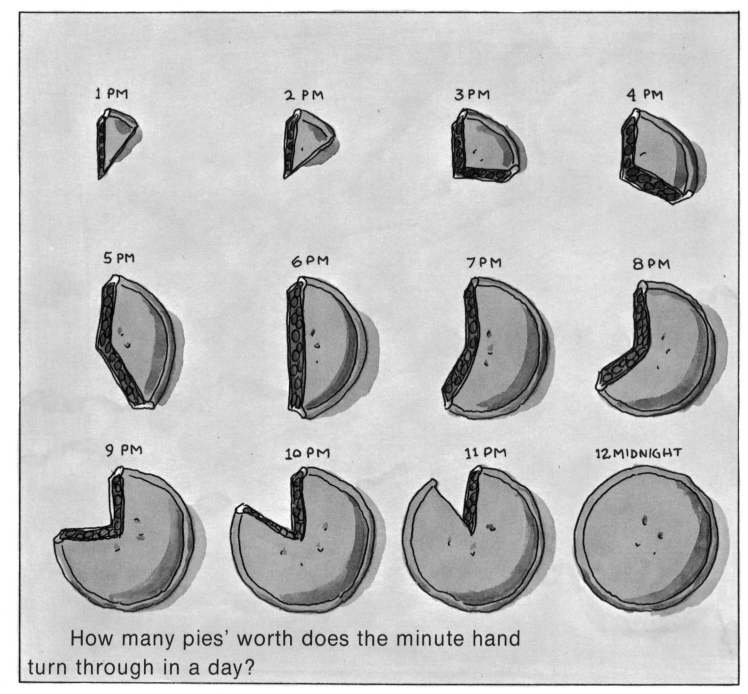

How many pies' worth does the minute hand turn through in a day?

Can you think of other things that turn
through a lot of pies' worth of angles?
How about the wheels of a car?

How about a ferris wheel?

Angles are easy as pie, and they can help you get to understand a lot of interesting things that go round and round.

ABOUT THE AUTHOR

This is Robert Froman's sixth book for the Young Math series. He says, "I always wanted to be a writer, and I had the luck to discover when I was a child that mathematics could be exciting, too. I like to pass that discovery along. The books I've done for the Young Math series are my favorite way of accomplishing this. What I've been trying to do in them is to make some of the basic ideas in mathematics both meaningful and intriguing to young readers."

ABOUT THE ILLUSTRATOR

Byron Barton, whose clever alligator appears on the pages of this book, has also illustrated many other books for children.

Mr. Barton was born in Pawtucket, Rhode Island. He has lived in Los Angeles, where he studied at the Chouinard Art Institute, and now makes his home in Greenwich Village in New York City.

M